Journeyman Electrician Exam Questions and Study Guide 2021

Learn All Secrets About the National Electrical Code

And Pass the Exam With No Effort

Experienced Trainers' Team

Table of Contents

Introduction

Become familiar with the NCE (National Electrical Code); the code has a language all its own. Understanding this language will help you to interpret the NEC better. Do not become intimidated by its length. Become thoroughly familiar with the definitions in chapter 1; if you don't, the remainder of the NEC will be difficult to comprehend. Remember, on the job, we use different "lingo" and phrases compared to the way the NEC is written and to the way many test questions are expressed.

Generally, electrician license candidates may not sit for an examination without submitting a completed license application (with all required documentation and applicable fees) to the state agency in which they are applying to take the examination. If the candidate is approved, they will be notified that they can schedule their examination.

Applicants will also be informed if their application is incomplete or does not satisfy the required criteria.

Most states require an applicant for the journeyman electrician license to have 8,000 hours (4 years) of on-the-job training under a master or journeyman electrician's supervision and pass a journeyman electrician examination. The examination is usually a 4-hour, 80-question multiple-choice test.

Generally, an applicant for the master electrician license must have 12,000 hours (6 years) of on-the-job training under the supervision of a master or journeyman electrician, hold a journeyman electrician license for 2 years, and pass a master electrician examination. Many states do require this criterion if one has a degree in electrical engineering. The examination is usually a 5-hour, 100-question multiple-choice test.

Please be advised, it is recommended that you first contact the state where you are applying for your license, because their specific requirements and criteria may vary.

Chapter 1:

Introduction to Journeyman Electrical Exam

When studying, get into the right frame of mind and relax. Study in a quiet place that is conducive to learning. If such a place is not available, go to your local library. It is important that you have the right atmosphere for studying. It is much better to study many short lengths of time than attempt to study fewer, longer lengths of time.

Try to study a little while, say about an hour, every evening. You will need the support and understanding of your family to set aside this much-needed time.

As you study these licensing exam preparation tests, the NEC, and other references, always highlight the important points. This makes it easier to locate the NEC references when taking the actual exam. Use a straight edge, such as a six-inch ruler when using the NEC tables and charts. A very common mistake is to get on the wrong line when using these tables. When that happens, the result is an incorrect answer. Use tabs on the major sections of your NEC so they are faster and easier to locate when taking the exam. The national average allowed per question is less than three minutes, you cannot waste time.

10

How to Take the Examination?

The journeyman electrician exam typically contains 80–100 questions and a 180–240-minute time limit.

That means, on average, you will only have three minutes to answer each question. The following instructions are especially important:

1. Before you open your code book or pick up a pencil, go through the entire exam and answer the questions you are confident you know. Mark all other questions so you can review them after you complete the first pass.

2. Next, go through the entire exam again. Mark for review any questions involving tables, motors, hazardous locations, calculations, and use your code book to answer the questions you think you know but were not sure about, such as definitions. Remember it is 3 minutes per question. Do not get hung up searching for answers! Check your time.

3. On your third pass, answer questions involving tables such as T.310.15(b) (16) for wire ampacity (T.310.16 in the 2020 NEC) transformer and motor questions.

Now you're ready to finish the exam. By this time, you should have about four minutes for each remaining question and have probably noticed a few questions that answered other questions from previous passes.

Commonly Used NEC Tables and Articles

Tbl. 110.26(A)(1)	Working Spaces About Electrical Equipment of 600 Volts or Less.
Tbl. 110.28	Enclosure Selection.
210.8	GFCI Protection for Personnel.
210.12	AFCI Protection.
Tbl. 210.21(B)(3)	Receptacle Ratings.
Tbl. 210.24	Branch-Circuit Requirements.
Tbl. 220.12	General Lighting Loads by Occupancy.
Tbl. 220.42	Lighting Load Demand Factors.
Tbl. 220.55	Demand Factors for Household Cooking Appliances.
Tbl. 220.56	Demand Factors for Commercial Kitchen Equipment.
Tbl. 220.84	Optional Calculation-Demand Factors for Multi-Family Dwellings.
240.6(A)	Standard Ampere Ratings of Overcurrent Protection Devices.
Tbl. 250.66	Grounding Electrode Conductor.
Tbl. 250.102(C)(1)	Grounded Conductors and Bonding Jumpers for AC Systems.
Tbl. 250.122	Equipment Grounding Conductors.

Chapter 2:

Preparations for the Journeyman Electrical Exam

T he following tests help to prepare students for the electricians' licensing exam. Most electrical exams consist of multiple-choice questions, and this is the type of questions reflected in these tests. The questions will give you a feel for how many of the examinations nationwide are structured. Remember that becoming familiar with the NEC language will help you to a better understanding of the subject.

Test Preparation Tips

- **Start studying 3 months before the test:** you have a lot of information to review to get prepared. Give yourself enough time to study all of it in a relaxed state of mind. Trying to cram your study in a month or a few weeks before the test will just create anxiety and even panic, which is not conducive to learning.

- **Outline a study schedule and stick to it:** you first need to find out what subjects the test covers, then break them down into a study outline. An outline of the material will give you a birds-eye-view of what you have to cover and allow you to plan actually to study it. Include review days throughout the schedule where you review material you studied the month or two before. Include practice test sessions in your schedule as well. Once you have a study schedule established, commit to it and be disciplined. It will help you and give you the benefit of comprehensive study if you actually follow it.

- **Study every day for at least one hour:** getting prepared for a professional certification exam takes commitment, and to maintain it, it is best to make it part of your regular schedule. Plan an hour a day to study the material you have scheduled for the day.

- **Obtain a good study guide:** a good study guide is very important. It will give you the substance you need to know for the test.

- **Use flashcards:** flashcards are easy to use and can interject some fun into the study process. Flashcards that give you a question on one side and an answer on the other are the most effective. Use them regularly throughout your study schedule.

- **Take untimed practice tests periodically to assess your knowledge of the material:** use the Tests.com practice test to find out how well you know the material. For the first couple of times, do not time yourself, but use the test simply to determine your strengths and weaknesses. Focus your study on the areas of the exam where you had the most trouble.

- **Take a timed practice test periodically to practice test-taking skills:** take the Tests.com practice test using a timer setting. Determine how many questions are on your state exam and complete that number of questions in the allotted time. This exercise will allow you to get a sense of how fast you need to work under time pressure.

- **Tab and highlight your reference books:** depending on the test, some jurisdictions have open book tests, allowing you to use a reference book while you take the test. Most testing rules do not allow notes in the reference book you use, but many allow highlighting and tabbing. When you use a reference book during a test, it is important to use it in such a way that allows you to work efficiently and not slow you down. Place colored tabs on the pages of the book referencing the sections, so you can turn to them quickly and not have to look up page numbers in the table of contents. Highlight those sections which you believe to be important and that will be subject to testing.

- **Meet with friends who are studying for the test and have a group discussion:** your friends and colleagues who are studying for the test will have different strengths and weaknesses than you. You can benefit each other by sharing information, discussing issues, and asking each other questions about the information subject to testing.

- **Don't study the day or night before the test:** you have to be prepared months in advance. Even though you may feel a bit anxious the day before the test, it is important that you give your brain a rest. During the test, you must be clear of mind and able to move from question to question nimbly. If your brain is tired and your eyes are having trouble focusing, you will put yourself at a great disadvantage. Do not study late into the night. You know the material more than you realize. Take the day off, go for a walk, a bike ride or see a movie.

Helpful Hints on Taking the Exam

- **Complete the easy questions first:** on most tests, all questions are valued the same. If you become too frustrated on any one question, it may reflect upon your entire test.

- **Keep track of time:** do not spend too much time on one question. If a question is difficult for you, mark the answer you think is correct and place a check ( ) by that question in the examination booklet. Then go on to the next question; if you have time after finishing the rest of the exam, you can go back to the questions you have checked. If you simply do not know the answer to a question, take a guess. Choose the answer that is most familiar to you. In most cases, the answer is B or C.

- **Only change answers if you know you are right:** usually, your first answer is your best answer.

- **Relax:** do not get uptight and stressed out when testing.

- **Tab your code book:** references are easier and faster to find.

- **Use a straightedge:** Prevent getting on the wrong line when referring to the tables in the NEC.

- **Understand the question:** one keyword in a question can make a difference in what the question is asking. Underlining keywords will help you to understand the meaning of the question.

- **Use a dependable calculator:** use a solar-powered calculator that has a battery back-up. Since many test sites are not well lighted, this type of calculator will prepare you for such a situation. If possible, bring along a spare calculator.

- **Show up at least 30 minutes prior to your exam time:** be sure to allow yourself time for traffic (among other things) when planning your route to the exam location.

Chapter 3:

Journeyman Electrical Exam Regulations in Various States

Most licensing agencies outsource their examinations to a testing agency that is a separate entity from the licensing agency. After you get approval from the licensing agency to take the exam, contact the testing agency for their regulations.

To ensure that all examinee are evaluated under equally favorable conditions, the following regulations and procedures are observed at most examination sites:

- Each examinee must present proper photo identification, preferably your driver's license before being allowed to take the test.

- No cameras, notes, tape recorders, pagers, or cellular phones are allowed in the examination room.

- No one will be permitted to work beyond the established time limits.

- Examinees are not permitted any reference material except the NEC.

- Examinees will be permitted to use noiseless calculators during the examination. Calculators that provide programmable ability or pre-programmed calculators are prohibited.

- Permission of an examination proctor must be obtained before leaving the room while the examination is in progress.

- Each examinee is assigned to a seat specifically designated by name and number when admitted to the examination room.

Chapter 4:

Electrical Analysis Techniques

Energy Sources

There are basically two types of energy sources: voltage source and current source. Again, they can be classified as ideal and practical sources. First, we'll discuss ideal sources then consider practical sources.

Voltage Source

An ideal voltage source is an energy source that gives constant voltage across its terminals irrespective of the current drawn by the load connected to its terminals. At any instant of time, the voltage across the terminals remains the same. Thus, the V-I characteristics of an ideal voltage source is a straight line as shown.

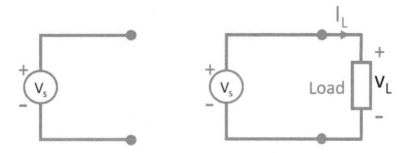

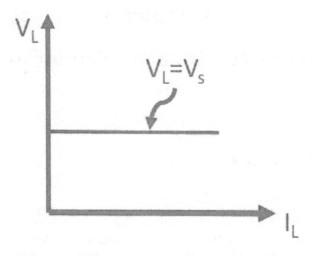

V-I Characteristics

But it is not possible to make such voltage sources in practice. Practically, all voltage sources have small internal resistance. For analysis purposes, we assume that this internal resistance is in series with the voltage source and is represented by R_{se}. Because of R_{se}, the voltage across the terminals decreases slightly with the increase in the current.

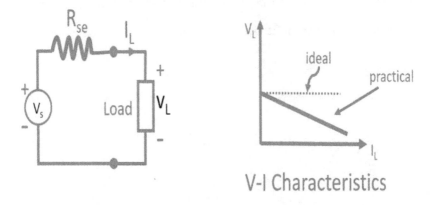

V-I Characteristics

$$V_L = V_S - I_L R_{se}$$

Usually, voltage sources are manufactured keeping the internal resistance to the minimum, such that it acts more or less like an ideal voltage source (till a max load current limit). Batteries are an example of the voltage source.

Current Source

No prizes for guessing what a current source is—an ideal current source is a power source that gives constant current, irrespective of the voltage appearing across its terminals.

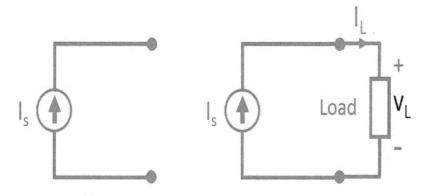

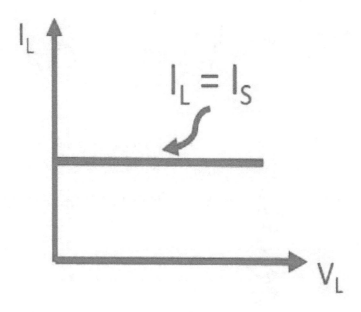

V-I Characteristics

But a practical current source hardly ever functions this way. In a practical current source, the current decreases slightly as the voltage across the load terminals increase. This behavior can be analyzed by considering a high internal resistance, represented by R_{sh} in parallel with the source.

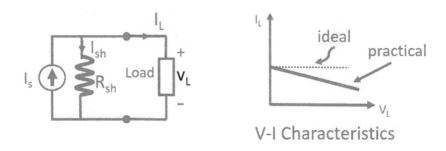

V-I Characteristics

$$I_L = I_s - \frac{V_L}{R_{sh}}$$

Combination of Sources

In many circuits, it is necessary to use multiple energy sources. Analyzing such circuits directly is a bit of a mess; so, what we usually do is to reduce the multiple sources to a single equivalent source, making the analysis a lot easier. Like the resistors and other circuit components, power sources too can have series or parallel combinations.

Combination of Voltage Sources

If two voltage sources are in series, i.e. they are connected back-to-back, the effective voltage is simply their algebraic sum. It is important to consider their polarities while doing so. If their polarities are the same, then the effective voltage is their sum; if their polarities are opposing, then the effective voltage is the difference between the 2 voltages.

Unlike a series connection, any two voltage sources can't be combined in parallel. Practically, only voltage sources of the same magnitude are combined in parallel. If 2 unequal voltage sources are connected in parallel, there will be a circulating current between them. Essentially, what happens is that the smaller voltage source is acting as a load for the larger voltage source. The magnitude of the current will depend on the value of the internal resistances of the 2 sources. Since the internal resistance is usually very small, a very large current flows, leading to overheating and possibly irreparable damage. Don't even think about connecting 2 ideal voltage sources in parallel—results could be catastrophic. And If you somehow manage to connect two voltage sources in parallel without damaging anything, the voltage across the combination will be somewhere between the 2 values depending on the internal resistances.

If 2 equal voltage sources are connected in parallel, the single equivalent source will have the same voltage as the 2 sources. The only reason to do this would be if the load requires a higher current than the source can supply by itself. Other than that, no good can come from connecting 2 voltage sources in parallel.

Combination of Current Sources

Connecting 2 current sources in series is a bit like connecting two voltage sources in parallel. It's simply not a good idea. There are very few cases where such connection is required in practice, but that's a rarity. In any case, only 2 current sources of the same magnitude are connected in series. The magnitude of the single equivalent source will supply the same current as the individual sources. Connecting 2 different current sources in series is a violation of Kirchhoff's current law. Again, you don't want to be messing with Kirchhoff! The problem with connecting 2 unequal current sources in series is that you are asking the small current source to supply more than it is capable of. Intuitively, this means one source is trying to push more charge than the other source is capable of accepting.

If two current sources are connected in parallel, the effective current output of the combination is their algebraic sum. If the sources are in opposite direction, then the single equivalent source will produce current in the direction of the larger current source.

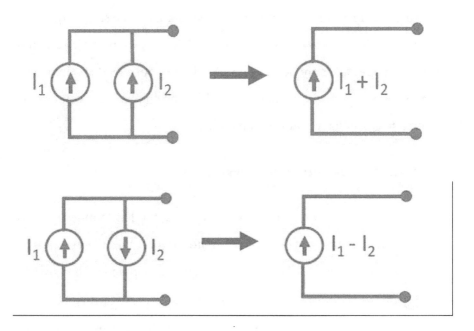

Source Transformation

In some circuits, you will encounter the presence of both current and voltage sources. This makes things a little trickier. Lucky for us, it is possible to convert one type of source to another type and it's pretty straightforward.

Consider a voltage source having an internal resistance R*se* connected to a load resistor R*L*. Now consider a current source having an internal resistance R*sh* supplying the same load. If the two supplies were to be equivalent, then the load current (or voltage) should be the same in both cases.

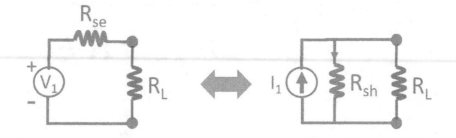

The current delivered by the voltage source is given by,

$$I = \frac{V_1}{R_{se} + R_L}$$

And the current delivered by the current source (applying current division rule) is given by,

$$I = I_1 \times \frac{R_{sh}}{R_{sh} + R_L}$$

Equating both equations,

$$\frac{V_1}{R_{se} + R_L} = I_1 \times \frac{R_{sh}}{R_{sh} + R_L}$$

Now if we equate the numerators and denominators separately, we get,

$$R_{se} = R_{sh}$$
$$\&$$
$$V_1 = I_1 R_{sh}$$

Once the sources are transformed into the same kind, they can be easily combined in series or parallel, as we did in the previous section.

Mesh Analysis

Using circuit analysis techniques, we are essentially trying to find the voltage across or current through a component in a circuit. Two of the most popular and basic analysis techniques are the node and the mesh analysis. These techniques were developed as an extension to the KVL and KCL. We'll learn about mesh analysis in this section and about the node analysis in the next.

In mesh analysis, we are dividing the circuit into areas or loops called meshes and assigning them a mesh current. Consider the circuit below; just from observation, we can identify 3 loops or meshes. Do note that these loops have some common components.

Now assume a loop current to flow in each of these loops and give them a random direction (although normally we assume clockwise direction as in the figure).

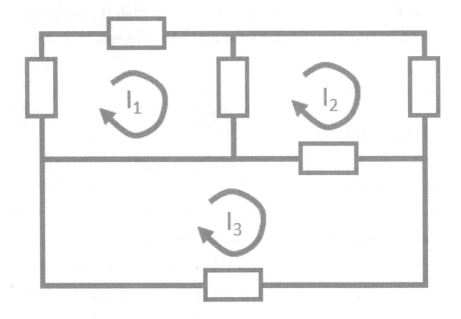

At first glance, this may seem like extra work, but it's worth it because reduces the number of equations significantly, making calculation very easy.

Now let's try out an example. Consider the circuit below, it has 2 voltage sources and a bunch of resistors. Simply through observation, we can identify 3 meshes. Let's assume currents IA, IB, IC flow through the 3 meshes respectively.

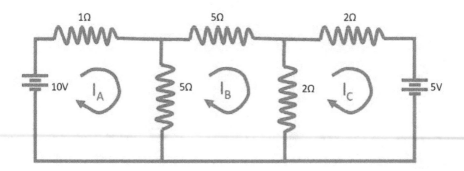

Now let's consider each mesh separately and form equations using KVL. Do note that the 5Ω resistor is common to both meshes A and B, so the current through it is the difference of the two mesh currents (because the currents are in opposite direction w.r.t 5Ω resistor.)

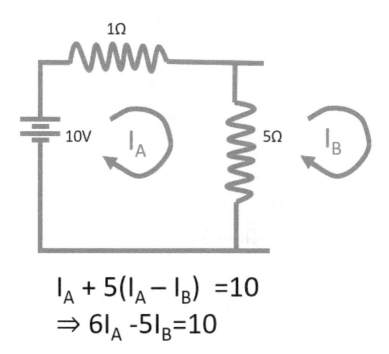

$$I_A + 5(I_A - I_B) = 10$$
$$\Rightarrow 6I_A - 5I_B = 10$$

Similarly, we form an equation for the other two meshes.

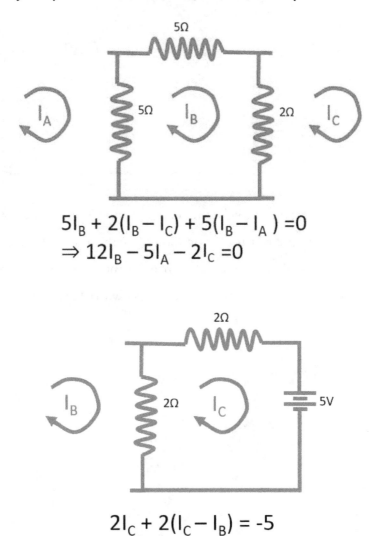

$$5I_B + 2(I_B - I_C) + 5(I_B - I_A) = 0$$
$$\Rightarrow 12I_B - 5I_A - 2I_C = 0$$

$$2I_C + 2(I_C - I_B) = -5$$
$$\Rightarrow 4I_C - 2I_B = -5$$

Super Mesh

Mesh analysis is all well and good, but what if a current source is present in the circuit? We could assign an unknown voltage across the current source, apply KVL around each mesh as before, and then relate the source current to the assigned mesh currents. This is generally the more difficult approach. The easier method is to create something called the super mesh, which is basically a mesh formed by combining 2 adjacent meshes, ignoring the branch which contains the current source.

For example, in the circuit below, we create a super mesh by combining meshes A and B. The super mesh equation can be obtained by applying KVL to the super mesh, ignoring the common branch (that contains the current source).

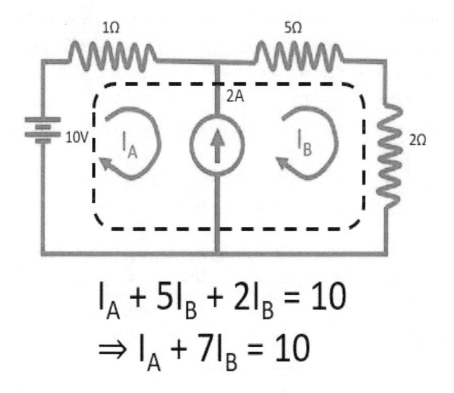

$$I_A + 5I_B + 2I_B = 10$$
$$\Rightarrow I_A + 7I_B = 10$$

The second equation relating the 2 mesh currents can be obtained by applying KCL to the common branch. In our example, it is,

$$I_B - I_A = 2$$

Nodal Analysis

Much like the mesh analysis, the nodal analysis is another commonly used circuit analysis technique. This analysis is based on KCL, whereas mesh analysis is based on KVL. Before we go any further, we need to define a node, which is simply a point where two or more circuit elements meet. Let's try using nodal analysis in practice. We'll use the same circuit we used in the mesh analysis example to get a better understanding between the similarities and differences between the two techniques.

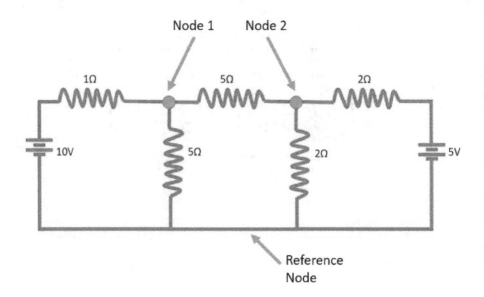

The first task in the nodal analysis is to identify the nodes in the circuit. Do note that in the nodal analysis we are only interested in nodes where 3 or more components meet. If we were to consider all the nodes, the method will still work, but the number of steps will increase. In our example, we can identify 3 such nodes. The next step is to assume one of those nodes as a reference node (usually, the bottom one is chosen). The idea is to assume zero voltage/potential at a point (reference node) in the circuit so that we can measure/calculate the voltage at different points with respect to this reference point. Once the reference node is fixed, assume voltages at the other nodes ($V1$, $V2$, $V3$, etc.) Once these values are taken care of, it's time to look at the nodes separately and form node equations.

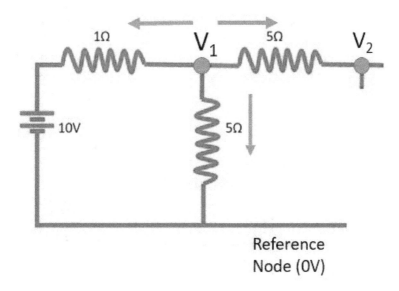

Reference Node (0V)

Applying KCL at node 1,

$$\frac{V_1 - 10}{1} + \frac{V_1}{5} + \frac{V_1 - V_2}{5} = 0$$

$$\Rightarrow 6V_1 - V_2 - 50 = 0$$

Similarly applying KCL at node 2,

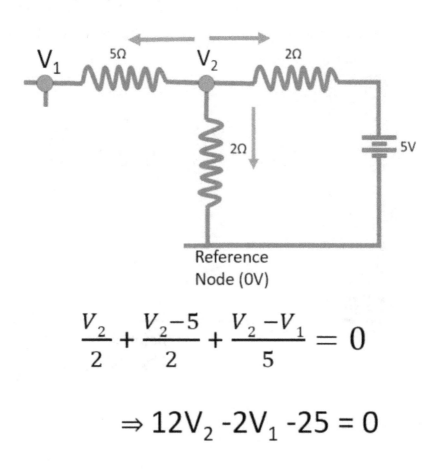

$$\frac{V_2}{2} + \frac{V_2 - 5}{2} + \frac{V_2 - V_1}{5} = 0$$

$$\Rightarrow 12V_2 - 2V_1 - 25 = 0$$

Solving these equations, we can obtain the node voltages and the rest of the parameters.

Chapter 5:

Common Electrical Formulas

Pie Circle Formulas

The PIE formula circle illustrates the relationship between power, current, and voltage. Power may be expressed as true power such as watts, kilowatts, kW, or horsepower.

It may also be expressed in terms of apparent power such as voltamps, VA, kilo voltamps, or kVA.

The letter "P" represents power.

The letter "I" represents current.

The letter "E" represents voltage.

The letter "k" is the abbreviation of kilo or one thousand (1,000).

One *kW* equals 1,000 watts.

One *kVA* equals 1,000 voltamps.

One horsepower equals 746 watts. Formulas used to determine the available power for a single-phase circuit, load or electrical system are the following:

$P = I \times E$.

P = current x volts.

P = volts x amps.

$P = VA$.

$P = kVA$.

kW = current x volts 1,000.

kVA = current x volts 1,000.

Example: determine the available power in VA for a 100-ampere, 240-volt, single-phase circuit.

A. 2,400 VA.

B. 24,000 VA.

C. 240,000 VA

D. 2.40 VA.

Answer: (B) 24,000 VA.

VA = I x E.

VA = 100 amperes x 240 volts = 24,000 VA.

Example: determine the apparent power in kVA for a 150-ampere, 120/240-volt, single-phase electrical system.

A. 36 kVA.

B. 3.60 kVA.

C. 360 kVA.

D. 3,600 kVA.

Answer: (A) 36 kVA.

kVA = I x E 1,000.

kVA = 150 amps x 240 volts = 36,000 = 36 kVA.

The formulas used to determine the available power for three-phase circuits, loads or electrical systems are the following:

P = I x E x 1.732.

P = current x volts x 1.732.

P = volts x 1.732 x amps.

P = VA x 1.732.

kW = current x volts x 1.732 1,000.

kVA = current x volts x 1.732 1,000.

Example: determine the available power, in VA, for a 100 ampere 208Y/120 volt, three-phase circuit.

A. 3,603 VA.

B. 36,026 VA.

C. 360,260 VA.

D. 20,800 VA.

Answer: (B)36,026 VA.

VA = I x E x 1.732.

VA = 100 amps x 208 volts x 1.732 = 36,026 VA.

Note: in this situation, we are to use 208 volts and multiply by 1.732 (the square root of 3), because we are to balance the load in the three current-carrying conductors.

Example: a load that draws 50 amperes when connected to a 208Y/120-volt, three-phase source has a kW rating of _____.

A. 18 kW.

B. 1.8 kW.

C. 180 kW.

D. 1,800 kW.

Answer: (A)18 kW.

kW = current x volts x 1.732.

kW = 50 x 208 x 1.732 = 18,013 = 18 kW.

Current may be expressed in terms such as amps, amperes, full load current, FLC, full load amps, FLA, load in amps *or* amperes, amperage, amperage draw, or line load.

The letter "I" represents the intensity of the current.

Formulas used to determine the current in a single-phase circuit, load, or electrical system are the following:

I = PE.

I = power voltage.

I = watts volts.

I = kW x 1,000 volts.

I = VA_volts.

I = kVA x 1,000 volts.

Example: determine the current in amperes for a 120-volt, single-phase branch circuit that has only six (6) 100-watt incandescent luminaires (lighting fixtures) connected.

A. 5 amperes.

B. 15 amperes.

C. 20 amperes.

D. 2 amperes.

Answer: (A) 5 amperes.

I = watts I = 600= 5 amperes volts 120.

Example: determine the current in amperes of a 2.4-kW load connected to a 240-volt, single-phase source.

A. 01 ampere.

B. 1 ampere.

C. 100 amperes.

D. 10 amperes.

Answer: (D) 10 amperes.

I = 2.4 kW x 1,000 240 = 2,400 = 10 amperes 240.

The formulas used to determine the current in a three-phase circuit, load, or electrical system are the following:

I = P_____ E x 1.732.

I = power___ volts x 1.732.

I = watts___ volts x 1.732.

I = kW x 1,000_ volts x 1.732.

I = VA_____ volts x 1.732.

I = kVA x 1,000_ volts x 1.732.

Example: a 36,026-VA load connected to a 208Y/120-volt, three-phase circuit will draw _____ of current per phase.

A. 10 amperes.

B. 173 amperes.

C. 250 amperes.

D. 100 amperes.

Answer: (D) 100 amperes.

I = VA____

E x 1.732.

I = 36,026 VA____ = 36,026_ = 100 amperes 208 volts x 1.732 360.25.

Example: a balanced 60-kVA load connected to a 480Y/277-volt three-phase electrical system will have a full load current draw of _____ per phase.

A. 72 amperes.

B. 125 amperes.

C. 720 amperes.

D. 80 amperes.

Answer: (A) 72 amperes.

I = kVA x 1,000_ volts x 1.732.

I = 60 kVA x 1,000_ = 60,000_ = 72 amperes 480 volts x 1.732 831.36.

Voltage Drop Formulas

Formula Definitions

VD= volts dropped from a circuit.

2 = multiplying factor for single-phase circuits. The 2 represents the conductor length in a single-phase circuit.

1.732 = multiplying factor for three-phase circuits. The square root of 3 represents the conductor length in a three-phase circuit. The only difference between the single-phase and three-phase formulas is that "1.732" has replaced "2."

K = approximate resistivity of the conductor per mil foot. A mil foot is a wire 1-foot-long and one mil in diameter (one thousandth of an inch). The approximate K value for copper wire is 12.9 ohms and for aluminum wire is 21.2 ohms per mil foot.

I = current or amperage draw of the load.

D = the distance from the source voltage to the load.

CM = circular mil area of the conductor. (Chapter 8, Table 8).

Note: when determining wire size, distance or current, VD is the actual volts that can be dropped from the circuit. The recommended percentage for a branch circuit is 3%. Example: 3% of 120 volts is 3.6 volts. Do not enter 3% in the VD position.

To find voltage drop in a single-phase circuit.

VD = 2 x K x I x D CM.

To find wire size in a single-phase circuit.

CM = 2 x K x I x D VD.

To find the distance in a single-phase circuit.

D = CM x VD_ 2 x K x I.

To find maximum current in amperes in a single-phase circuit.

I = CM x VD_ 2 x K x D.

Ohm's Law Circle Formulas

Ohm's law circle formula illustrates the relationship between voltage, current, and resistance.

The letter "E" represents electromotive force or voltage.

The letter "I" represents the intensity of the current.

The letter "R" represents the friction opposite the flow of electrons in a conductor and is known as resistance; the unit of measurement is the ohm.

In an alternate current circuit, factors that oppose current flow are conductor resistance, capacitive reactance, and inductive reactance. This total opposition to current flow is known as impedance and is also measured in ohms; the letter "Z" represents the impedance and may be substituted for the letter "R."

The formula used to determine the current flow in an electrical circuit or load when the resistance and voltage are known is the following:

$I = E\_ R.$

$I = volts\_\_\_\_ resistance.$

Example: a 120-volt circuit supplies an incandescent luminaire (lighting fixture) with a resistance of 200 ohms. Determine the current flow, in amperes, of the circuit.

A. 6.00 amperes.

B. 0.60 amperes.

C. 3.00 amperes.

D. 1.60 amperes.

Answer: (B) 0.60 amperes.

I = volts____ = 120 volts_ = 0.60 amperes resistance 200 ohms.

The formula used to determine the voltage or voltage drop in an electrical circuit when the current and resistance are known is the following:

E = I x R.

E = current x resistance.

Example: determine the voltage drop of two sizes 10-AWG copper conductors that supply a 16-ampere load located 100 feet from the voltage source. Given: The total resistance of the two conductors is 0.25 ohms.

A. 2.00 volts.

B. 0.40 volts.

C. 4.00 volts.

D. 40.00 volts.

Answer: (C) 4.00 volts.

$E = I \times R$

$E = 16$ amperes x .25 ohms = 4 volts.

The formula used to determine the resistance in an electrical circuit or load when the voltage and current are known is the following:

$R = E\_ I.$

$R =$ voltage current.

Example: determine the resistance of the heating elements of an electric baseboard heater that draws 8 amperes when supplied from a 120-volt source.

A. 0.07 ohms.

B. 960 ohms.

C. 15 ohms.

D. 150 ohms.

Answer: (C)15 ohms.

$R =$ volts__ = 120 volts_ = 15 ohms current 8 amperes.

Chapter 6:

Understanding the Branch Circuits

U pon successfully completing this unit, the student will be familiar with the concept of sizing, rating, and overcurrent protection of branch circuits as well as calculating the number required.

# of circuits = load va circuit va

The definition of a branch circuit is the circuit conductors between the final overcurrent device (circuit breaker or fuse) protecting the circuit and the outlet(s). [Article 100] In other words, that portion of a wiring system that is beyond the final overcurrent device protecting the circuit and the outlet(s).

The rating of a branch circuit is determined by the maximum ampere rating of the overcurrent protective device (circuit breaker or fuse) and not by the size of the conductors used for the branch circuit. [210.3]

In general, branch circuit conductors must have an allowable ampacity (current-carrying capacity) of not less than 125% of the continuous load, plus 100% of the noncontinuous load to be served. [210.19(A)(1)(a)]

Example: when a single branch circuit serves a continuous load of 20 amperes and a noncontinuous load of 10 amperes, the branch circuit conductors are required to have an allowable current-carrying capacity of at least _____.

A. 30.00 amperes.

B. 37.50 amperes.

C. 35.00 amperes.

D. 32.50 amperes.

Answer: (C) 35.00 amperes.

20 amperes x 1.25 = 25 amperes.

10 amperes x 1.00 = 10 amperes total = 35 amperes.

The definition of a continuous load is a load where the maximum current is expected to continue for 3 hours or more. [Article 100]

Examples of continuous loads are lighting loads for commercial and industrial occupancies that are expected to be operated for at least 3 hours.

Examples of noncontinuous loads are general-purpose receptacle outlets provided for commercial, industrial, and residential occupancies and general-purpose lighting loads for residential occupancies.

In general, overcurrent devices protecting branch circuits will have a rating of not less than 125% of the continuous load to be served plus 100% of the noncontinuous load to be served. [210.20(A)] In other words, overcurrent devices protecting branch circuits are not to be loaded more than 80% of their rated value when protecting continuous loads.

Example: when a 100-ampere rated circuit breaker is used to protect a branch circuit serving a continuous load, the load shall not exceed _____.

A. 80 amperes.

B. 100 amperes.

C. 125 amperes.

D. 115 amperes.

Answer: (A) 80 amperes.

100 amperes x .80 = 80 amperes.

Note the exception to 210.20(A). If the overcurrent device protecting the circuit is listed for continuous operation, it will be permitted to have a rating of 100% of the continuous load(s) to be served. Be advised, circuit breakers are not listed for continuous operation unless they have a rating of at least 400 amperes or more.

In general, branch circuit loads must be calculated as shown in 220.12, 220.14, and 220.16 [220.10]

In general, lighting loads are to be supplied by 15-and 20-ampere rated branch circuits. [210.23(A)]

Lighting loads for specific occupancies must be based on the unit load per square foot depending on the type of occupancy as given in Table 220.12. below.

Table 220.12 General lighting loads by occupancy, type of occupancy, armories, and auditoriums.

Unit load volt-amperes per square meter: 11.

Volt-amperes per square foot: 1.

- Banks 39 _b_ 3½_b._
- Barber shops and beauty parlors 33 3.

- Churches 11 1.

- Clubs 22 2.

- Court rooms 22 2.

- Dwelling units 33 3.

- Garages, commercial (storage) 6 ½.

- Hospitals 22 2.

- Hotels and motels, including apartment houses without provision for cooking by tenants 22 2.

- Industrial commercial (loft) buildings 22 2.

- Lodge rooms 17 1½.

- Office buildings 39 *b* 3½*b.*

- Restaurants 22 2.

- Schools 33 3.

- Stores 33 3.

- Warehouses (storage) 3 ¼.

- Assembly halls and auditoriums 11 1.

- Halls, corridors, closets, stairways 6 ½.

- Storage spaces 3 ¼ *a* See 220.14(J) *b* See 220.14(K).

General lighting loads are to be calculated from the outside dimensions of the building. [220.12] To determine the area, in square feet, of a building, simply multiply the length of the building by the width of the building.

Example: a building has outside dimensions of 100 feet in length and 75 feet in width. The building has a total area of _____.

A. 750 square feet.

B. 175 square feet.

C. 7,500 square feet.

D. 1,750 square feet.

Answer: (C) 7,500 sq. ft.

100 ft. x 75 ft. = 7,500 sq. ft.

When calculating the area, in square feet, of a multi-story building, multiply the length of the building by the width of the building by the number of stories.

Example: a three (3) story building having outside dimensions of 100 feet by 75 feet has a total area of _____.

A. 2,225 square feet.

B. 7,500 square feet.

C. 15,000 square feet.

D. 22,500 square feet.

Answer: (D) 22,500 sq. ft.

100 ft. x 75 ft. x 3 (stories) = 22,500 sq. ft.

When calculating lighting loads for dwelling units, do not include open porches, garages, or unfinished spaces not adaptable for future use. [220.12]

Remember, in general, lighting loads for habitable spaces of dwelling units and guest rooms of hotels and motels are not considered as continuous use. But lighting loads of commercial and industrial occupancies are considered as continuous use.

The formula used to determine the minimum number of general lighting branch circuits required for a dwelling unit is the following:

Number of circuits = load VA_

Example: a dwelling unit having 2,000 sq. ft. of habitable space is required to have at least _____ 15-ampere, 120-volt general-purpose lighting branch circuits.

A. two.

B. three.

C. four.

D. five.

Answer: (C) four.

2,000 sq. ft. x 3 VA__ = 6,000 VA = 3.3 = 4 circuits 120 volts x 15 amperes 1,800 VA.

When calculating branch circuits, when your calculation results in decimal numbers, ex. 3.3, you must go to the next whole number. In other words, you cannot install part of a circuit or circuit breaker.

Apartment dwellings without provisions for cooking by tenants are to be calculated at the same value, 2 VA per square foot, like hotels and motels, when determining the minimum of general lighting branch circuits required for the living units. [Table 220.12]

Example: an apartment complex, without cooking facilities provided for the tenants, having 12,000 sq. ft. of living area, is required to have at least _____ 20 tenants, having 12,000 sq. ft. of living area, is required to have at least _____ 20-volt general lighting branch circuits.

A. ten–ten.

B. fourteen–fourteen.

C. ten–thirteen.

D. ten–fourteen.

Answer: (D) ten–fourteen.

12,000 sq. ft. x 2 VA_ = 24,000 VA = 10 circuits 120 volts x 20 amperes 2,400 VA.

12,000 sq. ft. x 2 VA = 24,000 VA = 13.3 = 14 circuits.

120 volts x *15* amperes 1,800 VA

A formula used to determine the minimum number of required general lighting branch circuits for an office building, store, bank, restaurant, *etc.* is the following:

Number of circuits = load VA x 125%

Example: a 10,000 sq. ft. restaurant is required to be provided with at least _____ 20-ampere, 120-volt general lighting branch circuits.

A. eight.

B. nine.

C. ten.

D. eleven.

Answer: (D) eleven.

10,000 x 2 VA x *125%* = 25,000 VA = 10.4 = 11 circuits 120 volts x 20 amps 2,400 VA.

Because the circuit breakers protecting the branch circuits are not permitted to be loaded to more than 80% of their rated value, [210.20(A)] we can also use these formulas:

Number of circuits = load VA_____ circuit VA x 80%

Number of circuits = 10,000 x 2 VA_ = 20,000 VA = 10.4 = 11 circuits 120 x 20 x 80% 1,920 VA.

Chapter 7:

Calculating Demand Loads for Cooking Equipment and Appliances Demand Loads

U pon successfully completing this unit, the student will be familiar with the concept of calculating demand loads for household cooking equipment and appliances.

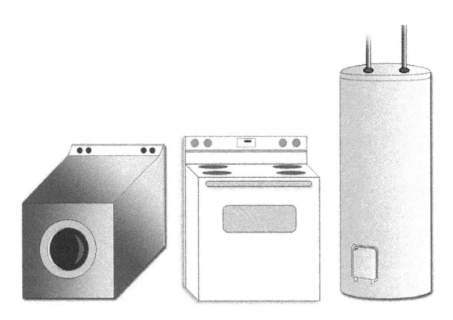

The definition of demand factor is the ratio of the maximum demand of a system, or part of a system, to the total connected load of a system or the part of the system under consideration. [Article 100]

The demand load of an electrical system or an electrical appliance is the maximum load of the system or appliance that may be required at a given time. In other words, demand factors are applied because all of the electrical loads are not used at the same time; all of the luminaires (lighting fixtures) will not be on at the same time, neither will all the receptacle outlets and appliances be fully loaded at the same time.

Demand factor (Percent) (See Notes)

Number of appliances	Column A (Less than 3½ kW Rating)	Column B (3½ kW to 8¾ kW Maximum Demand (kW)	Column C (Not over 12 kW Rating)
1	80	80	8
2	75	65	11
3	70	55	14
4	66	50	17
5	62	45	20
6	59	43	21

7	56	40	22
8	53	36	23
9	51	35	24
10	49	34	25
11	47	32	26
12	45	32	27
13	43	32	28
14	41	32	29
15	40	32	30
16	39	28	31
17	38	28	32
18	37	28	33
19	36	28	34
20	35	28	35
21	34	26	36
22	33	26	37
23	32	26	38
24	31	26	39
25	30	26	40
26-30	30	26	41

31-40	30	26	42
41-50	30	26	43
51-60	30	26	44
61 and over	30	26	45

Take notice that household electric ranges having a rating of 8.75 kW or more are required to be supplied by at least a 40-ampere rated branch circuit. [210.19(A)(3)] Therefore, demand factors are not to be applied when sizing branch circuits for these single cooking units.

Over 12 kW through 27 kW ranges all of the same ratings. For ranges individually rated more than 12 kW but not more than 27 kW, the maximum demand in column C must be increased 5% for each additional kilowatt of rating or major fraction thereof by which the rating of individual ranges exceeds 12 kW.

Over 8¾ kW through 27 kW ranges of unequal ratings. For ranges individually rated more than 8¾ kW and of different ratings, but none exceeding 27 kW, an average value of rating must be calculated by adding together the ratings of all ranges to obtain the total connected load (using 12 kW for any range rated less than 12 kW) and dividing by the total number of ranges. Then the maximum demand in column C must be increased 5% for each kilowatt or major fraction thereof by which this average value exceeds 12 kW.

Over 1¾ kW through 8¾ kW. In lieu of the method provided in column C, it can be permissible to add the nameplate ratings of all household cooking appliances rated more than 1¾ kW, but not more than 8¾ kW, and multiply the sum by the demand factors specified in column A and column B for the given number of appliances. Where the rating of cooking appliances falls under both column A and column B, the demand factors for each column will be applied to the appliances for that column, and the results added together.

Branch circuit load: It must be permissible to calculate the branch-circuit load for one range in accordance with Table 220.55. The branch circuit load for one wall-mounted oven or one counter-mounted cooking unit must be the nameplate rating of the appliance. The branch circuit load for a counter-mounted cooking unit and not more than two wall-mounted ovens, all supplied from a single branch circuit and located in the same room, must be calculated by adding the nameplate rating of the individual appliances and treating this total as equivalent to one range.

This table also applies to household cooking appliances rated over 1¾ kW and used in instructional programs.

Kitchen Equipment

For electric kitchen equipment in commercial occupancies, the branch circuits and overcurrent protection are sized according to the nameplate rating on the appliance. When sizing feeder and service conductors, the demand factors shown in Table 220.56 may be applied. However, the feeder or service demand load is not permitted to be less than the sum of the 2 largest kitchen equipment loads. [220.56]

Example: a catering service is to have the following cooking related equipment in the kitchen:

Water heater—5.5 kW booster heater—7.0 kW dishwasher—2.0 kW sterilizer—2.5 kW oven—6.0 kW grill—5.0 kW mixer—3.0 kW freezer—3.5 kW refrigerator—2.5 kW.

What is the demand load in kW on the service entrance conductors for the appliances?

A. 37.00 kW.

B. 25.90 kW.

C. 13.00 kW.

D. 24.05 kW.

Answer: (D) 24.05 kW.

Water heater—5.5 kW.

Booster heater—7.0 kW.

Dishwasher—2.0 kW.

Sterilizer—2.5 kW.

Oven—6.0 kW.

Grill—5.0 kW.

Mixer—3.0 kW.

Freezer—3.5 kW.

Refrigerator—2.5 kW.

(Connected load) 37 kW.

(Demand) x 65 % [Table 220.56] Demand Load = 24.05 kW.

Laundry Equipment

The branch-circuit conductors and overcurrent protection for laundry equipment in commercial occupancies are to be sized in accordance with the appliance nameplate rating. The NEC does not permit a demand factor to be applied to service, feeder, or branch-circuit conductors for commercial laundry equipment. Therefore, the laundry equipment demand load is to be calculated at 100%.

Example: the laundry room of a multifamily dwelling will have installed the following laundry equipment:

2–clothes dryers–7,000 VA each 3–washing machines–1,920 VA each 3–washing machines–1,500 VA each.

What is the demand load in VA on the service and feeder conductors for the listed appliances?

A. 24,260 VA.

B. 18,500 VA.

C. 16,982 VA.

D. 14,000 VA.

Answer: (A) 24,260 VA

Clothes dryers–2 x 7,000 VA = 14,000 VA.

Washing machine–3 x 1,920 VA = 5,760 VA.

Washing machine–3 x 1,500 VA = 4,500 VA.

Total = 24,260 VA.

Mobile Home and Manufactured Home Parks

The distribution system to mobile home lots is required to be 120/240-volts, single-phase. [550.30] Because appliances, luminaries, and other equipment volts single-phase; three-phase systems and systems of a different voltage would not be compatible with the loads to be supplied.

Each mobile home lot is required to be calculated on the basis of the larger of a minimum of not less than 16,000 VA for each mobile home lot, or to the calculated load of the largest typical mobile home the lot will accommodate. [550.31] However, for each mobile home to be served, the service equipment is to be rated at least 100 amperes, [550.32(C)] and the mobile home lot feeder conductors must have a current-carrying capacity (ampacity) of not less than 100 amperes. [550.33(B)]

When sizing service-entrance conductors for a mobile home park, the demand factors, based on the number of mobile homes in the park, displayed in Table 550.31 are permitted to be applied.

Example: what is the minimum demand load in amperes on the service conductors of a mobile home park consisting of 15 lots?

A. 250 amperes.

B. 260 amperes.

C. 400 amperes.

D. 1,000 amperes.

Answer: (B) 260 amperes.

15 lots x 16,000 VA (MINIMUM) = 240,000 VA

Demand = x .26 [Tbl. 550.31] demand load = 62,400 VA

$I = P \div E$

$I = 62,400$ VA = 260 amperes

Example: a twenty-five-lot mobile home park is to be constructed. Each lot in the park is capable of accommodating a mobile home with a rating of 24,000 VA. Determine the demand load, in amperes, on the park service conductors.

A. 1,000 amperes.

B. 650 amperes.

C. 400 amperes.

D. 600 amperes.

Answer: (D) 600 amperes.

25 lots x 24,000 VA = 600,000 VA.

x.24 [Tbl.550.31]

Demand load = 144,000 VA.

$I = P \div E$

I = 144,000 VA = 600 amperes 240 volts.

Chapter 8:
Determining the Ampacity of Conductors

U pon successfully completing this unit, the student will be familiar with the concept of determining the ampacity of conductors, application of correction factors, proper sizing, and insulation ratings of conductors.

Required ampacity =Load correction factors.

The definition of ampacity is the maximum current, in amperes, that a conductor can carry continuously under the conditions of use without exceeding its temperature rating.

[Article 100] To get a better understanding of ampacity, perhaps we might consider it as current-carrying capacity, or the maximum amperage a conductor can carry without damaging the conductor and its insulation.

When determining the ampacity of a conductor, or sizing a conductor, there are several factors needed to be taken into consideration, such as the ambient temperature, the type and temperature rating of the conductor insulation, the number of current-carrying conductors contained in the raceway or cable, the temperature rating of the terminations, characteristics of the load to be served, the environment the conductor will be subject to and voltage drop, which will be discussed later.

Temperature rating of conductor (See Table 310.104(A) 60° C

Temperature rating of conductor
(140° F) 75° C (167° F) 90° C (194° F)
60° C (140° F) 75° C (167° F) 90° C (194° F)
Types RHW, THHW, THW, Types THWN, XHHW, TW, UF USE, ZW
Types TBS, SA, SIS, FEP, FEPB, MI, RHH, RHW2, THHN, THHW, THW-2, THWN-2,
USE-2, XHH, XHHW, XHHW-2, ZW-2
Types TW, UF
Types RHW, THHW, THW THWN, XHHW, USE Types TBS, SA, SIS, THHN, THHW, THW-2, THWN-2, RHH, RHW-2, USE-2, XHH, XHHW, XHHW-2, ZW-2
Size
AWG or COPPER**kcmil**
Size ALUMINUM OR COPPER-CLADAWG or ALUMINUMkcmil
18 - -
16 - -
14** 15 20
12** 20 25
10** 30 35 8 40 50 14 18 25 30 40 55

- - - -
- - - -
- - - - 15 20 25 12** 25 30 35 10** 35 40 45 8
6 55 65
4 70 85
3 85 100
2 95 115
1 110 130 75 95 115 130 145 40 50 55 6 55 65 75 4 65 75 85 3 75 90 100 2 85 100 115 1
1/0 125 150
2/0 145 175
3/0 165 200
4/0 195 230
170 195 225 260 100 120 135 1/0 115 135 150 2/0 130 155 175 3/0 150 180 205 4/0
250 215 255
300 240 285
350 260 310
400 280 335
500 320 380
290 320 350 380 430 170 205 230 250 195 230 260 300 210 250 280 350 225 270 305 400 260 310 350 500 600 350 420
700 385 460
750 400 475
800 410 490

900 435 520
475 520 535 555 585 285 340 385 600 315 375 425 700 320 385 435 750 330 395 445 800 355 425 480 900
1000 455 545
1250 495 590
1500 525 625
1750 545 650
2000 555 665
615 665 705 735 750 375 445 500 1000 405 485 545 1250 435 520 585 1500 455 545 615 1750 470 560 630 2000

Refer to 310.15 (B)(2) for the ampacity correction factors where the ambient temperature is other than 30° C (86° F). Refer to 240.4 (D) for conductor overcurrent protection limitations.

The temperature rating of a conductor is the maximum temperature, at any location along its length, that the conductor can withstand over a prolonged period of time without serious damage occurring. [310.15(A)(3), INF. Note #1]

When conductors are subject to ambient temperatures above 86° F, the resistance of the conductors is also increased proportionately. The greater the elevated ambient temperature, the greater the resistance. When the resistance of a conductor increases, the ampacity of the conductor decreases. When this condition occurs, you must apply the appropriate temperature correction factors given in Table 310.15(B)(2)(a).

Ambient temperature rating of conductor. (°C) Temp. (°F) 60° C 75°C 90° C

Ambient (°C)	60°C	75°C	90°C	Temp. (°F)
10 or less	1.29	1.20	1.15	50 or less
11-15	1.22	1.15	1.12	51-59
16-20	1.15	1.11	1.08	60-68
21-25	1.08	1.05	1.04	69-77
26-30	1.00	1.00	1.00	78-86
31-35	0.91	0.94	0.96	87-95
36-40	0.82	0.88	0.91	96-104
41-45	0.71	0.82	0.87	105-113
46-50	0.58	0.75	0.82	114-122
51-55	0.41	0.67	0.76	123-131
56-60	-	0.58	0.71	132-140
61-65	-	0.47	0.65	141-149
66-70	-	0.33	0.58	150-158
71-75	-	-	0.50	159-167

76-80 - - 0.41 168-176

81-85 - - 0.29 177-185

Example: when a size 3 AWG copper conductor, with THW insulation, is installed in an area where the ambient temperature is 114 deg. F, the wire has an allowable ampacity of _____.

A. 100 amperes.

B. 75 amperes.

C. 82 amperes.

D. 58 amperes.

Answer: (B) 75 amperes.

100 amperes x .75 = 75 amperes.

To solve this problem, first, we locate the wire size on the left side of Table 310.15(B) (16) and look to the right under the copper THW column, with a temperature rating of 75° C, and note the ampacity of the wire is 100 amperes at normal operating temperature. Then, we apply the values as shown in Table 310.15(B)(2)(a). Look to the right side of the table where the ambient temperature is shown as °F and find the ambient temperature. Next, we follow that line to the left where the line intersects with the 75° C column (temperature rating of the conductor) to find our correction factor of .75 or 75%. Finally, to find the allowable ampacity of the conductor, multiply the two values together.

Example: when a size 1/0 AWG THWN aluminum conductor is installed at an ambient temperature of 45° C, the conductor has an allowable ampacity of _____.

A. 100 amperes.

B. 90 amperes.

C. 98 amperes.

D. 104 amperes.

Answer: (C) 98 amperes.

1/0 THWN aluminum ampacity before derating = 120 amperes 120 amps x .82 (correction factor) = 98.4 amperes.

We use the same steps as before. First, we find the wire size which has an ampacity of 120 amperes. [Tbl. 310.15(B)(16)] Then, we find the ambient temperature, this time on the left portion of Table 310.15(B)(2)(a), and go to the right under the THWN aluminum column (temperature rating of conductor) to find the correction factor of 82.

Next, multiply the two values together. The temperature correction factors in Table 310.15(B)(2)(a) are to be applied when sizing conductors for a given load located in an area with an elevated ambient temperature. The formula that should be used is the following:

Required ampacity = load_____ correction factor.

Example: where a 100-ampere load is to be supplied with THWN copper conductors in an area where the ambient temperature will reach 110° F, size _____ THWN conductors are required to serve the load.

A. 1 AWG.

B. 2 AWG.

C. 3 AWG.

D. 1/0 AWG.

Answer: (A) 1 AWG.

Required ampacity = 100 amps = 122 amperes .82

Table 310.15(B) (16) indicates size 1 AWG copper conductors with an ampacity of 130 amperes, should be selected. To cross-reference:

130 amperes x .82 (correction factor) = 107 amperes

Conductors are to be sized in accordance with the lowest temperature rating of the terminal, device, or conductor of the circuit. [110.14(C)] In other words, conductors must be sized to the lowest temperature rating of the wire, circuit breaker, terminal, or device.

Conductors with temperature ratings higher than that of the terminations are permitted to be used for ampacity adjustment and correction. [110.14(C)] Today, most terminations are rated at 60° C or 75° C.

This permits us to use THHN conductors for derating purposes, but the conductor size is based on the lower terminal rating of the circuit breaker, equipment, or device, not the 90° C rating of the conductor insulation.

Example: the load on a size 6 AWG THHN copper conductor is limited to _____ where connected to a circuit breaker with a termination rated at 60° C.

A. 75 amperes.

B. 65 amperes.

C. 60 amperes.

D. 55 amperes.

Answer: (D) 55 amperes.

Table 310.15(B)(16) lists the ampacity of size 6 AWG, copper, 60° C rated conductors to be 55 amperes.

Example: the load, in amperes, on a size 6 AWG THHN copper conductor is permitted to be no more than _____ where connected to a fusible disconnect switch with terminals rated at 75° C.

A. 75 amperes.

B. 65 amperes.

C. 60 amperes.

D. 55 amperes.

Answer: (B) 65 amperes.

Chapter 9:

How to Size Electrical Boxes

Raceways

U pon successfully completing this unit, the student will be familiar with the concept of properly sizing electrical boxes and raceways.

Number of wires permitted =Allowable fill wire size.

Outlet and Device Box Sizing

Device and junction boxes are required to be of sufficient size to house conductors and devices, clamps, and support fittings without damaging the conductor's insulation. Therefore, when sizing boxes, conductors, clamps, and support fittings are required to be counted in order to select the proper size box. To properly size outlet boxes, you must count the conductors within the box correctly. Section 314.16(B)(1) is to be used as a guideline to count the conductors as follows:

- Conductors that originate outside the box or that are spliced within the box are counted one for each conductor.

- Conductors unbroken within the box, less than 12 inches in length, that pass through the box without splicing or terminating are counted one for each conductor.

- Conductors 12 inches or longer that are looped and unbroken are counted as two for a single conductor.

- Conductors that originate within the box and do not leave the box such as, bonding jumpers and pigtails are not counted.

- Conductors from a domed luminaire (fixture) that terminate within the box are not counted.

When sizing devices and junction boxes, the insulation of the conductors is not required to be taken into consideration. The volume required for the individual conductors is expressed in cubic inches and cubic centimeters, no matter what the insulation characteristics of the conductor(s) are/are.

To determine the volume, in cubic inches, of a box simply multiply the length times the width times the depth of the box.

Example: a box that measures 6 inches x 6 inches and is 4 inches deep has a volume of _____.

A. 96 cubic inches.

B. 144 cubic inches.

C. 24 cubic inches.

D. 36 cubic inches.

Answer: (B) 144 cubic inches.

6 in. x 6 in. x 4 in. = 144 cubic inches.

Table 314.16(A) may be used to determine the minimum size outlet box required for a given number of conductors, or when determining the maximum number of conductors permitted in an outlet box when all of the conductors in the box are of the same size.

Example: determine the maximum number of size 12 AWG THWN conductors permitted in a 4-x 1½ in. square box.

A. seven.

B. eight.

C. nine.

D. ten.

Answer: (C) nine.

The right-hand side of Table 314.16(B) under the 12 column shows nine conductors permitted in the box.

Example: in the following list, which one of the boxes is the minimum required to house three size 12 AWG THWN/THHN conductors and three sizes 12 AWG THW conductors?

A. 4 x 1½ in. octagon.

B. 4 x 2¼ in. octagon.

C. 4 x 1½ in. square.

D. 4 x 2¼ in. square.

Answer: (A) 4 x 1½ in. octagon.

Table 314.16(B) permits six sizes 12 AWG conductors in a 4-x 1½ in. octagon box.

Table 314.16(A) must apply where no fittings or devices, such as cable clamps, luminaire studs, hickeys, receptacles, switches, or dimmers, are enclosed in the box. Table 314.16(A) does not take into consideration the fill requirements for these fittings or devices; where one or more of these items are contained in the box, the number of conductors permitted, as shown in the table, will be reduced as follows:

- **Cable clamps:** one or more internal cable clamps present in the box are counted as one conductor, based on the largest conductor in the box. [314.16(B)(2)]

- **Support fittings:** one or more luminaire (fixture) studs and hickeys in the box are counted as one conductor for each type of fitting, based on the largest conductor in the box. [314.16(B)(3)]

- **Devices:** for each yoke or strap containing one or more devices present in the box, they are to be counted as two wires, based on the largest conductor connected to the device. [314.16(B)(4)]

- **Equipment grounding conductors:** one or more equipment grounding conductors or bonding jumpers contained in a box are to be counted as one conductor, based on the largest equipment grounding conductor or bonding jumper in the box. [314.16(B)(5)] Where an additional set of isolated equipment grounding conductors are in the box, they are to be counted as one conductor, based on the largest equipment grounding conductor in the additional set.

When doing box fill calculations, we must take into consideration the volume taken up by all conductors, fittings, and devices contained in the box to properly size the box.

Example: a device box contains 2 internal clamps, 2 equipment grounding conductors, 1 bonding jumper, and 1 duplex receptacle. The number of conductors permitted in the box is to be reduced by _____ conductors.

A. three.

B. four.

C. five.

D. six.

Answer: (B) four.

Clamps = 1 wire receptacle = 2 wires equip. grounding & bonding wires = 1 wire.

Total = 4 wires

When calculating the proper size outlet box to be used when the conductors are of different sizes, you are to determine the volume of the conductors, in cubic inches, by applying Table 314.16(B), and then size the box by using Table 314.16(A).

Example: determine which one of the following listed outlet boxes is the minimum size required to enclose the following conductors:

Six sizes 12 AWG conductors.

Two sizes 14 AWG conductors.

One size 14 AWG equipment grounding conductors.

A. 4 x 1½ in. octagon.

B. 4 x 1½ in. square.

C. 4 x 2¼ in. square.

D. 4¼ x 1½ in. square.

Answer: (B) 4 x 1½ in. square.

Size 12 AWG = 2.25 cu. in. x 6 Size 14 AWG = 2.00 cu. in. x 2 Size 14 AWG Equip. grounding x 1 = 13.5 cubic inches = 4.0 cubic inches = 2.0 cubic inches_

19.5 cubic inches

Table 314.16(A) requires a 4-x 1½ inch square box having a volume of 21 cubic inches.

Junction and Pull Box Sizing

In straight pulls, the length of the box must not be less than eight times the trade diameter of the largest raceway entering the box. [314.28(A)(1)]

Example: determine the minimum length of a pull box that has a trade size 3½ inch conduit entering at each end, and containing conductors of size 250 kcmil, when a straight pull of the conductors is to be made.

A. 21 inches

B. 24 inches

C. 28 inches

D. 32 inches

Answer: (C) 28 inches.

3.5 in. (conduit) x 8 = 28 inches

Where splices, angles, or U-pulls are made, the distance between each raceway entry inside the box and opposite wall of the box must not be less than 6 times the trade size of the raceway in a row [314.28(A)(2)]. Then, you are to add the sum of the trade size diameter of any additional raceways entering the box. In other words, for angle or U-pulls, the proper size junction box can be determined by multiplying the largest raceway by 6 and add any additional conduits.

Example: a junction box is to be installed where the conductors are larger than size 4 AWG and an angle (90 deg.) pull of the conductors is to be made. 2 trade size 3-inch conduits are to enter the box from the top and 2 trade size 3-inch conduits are to enter the box from the side. Determine the minimum size pull box required.

A. 36 in. x 36 in.

B. 27 in. x 27 in.

C. 24 in. x 24 in.

D. 21 in. x 21 in.

Answer: (D) 21 in. x 21 in.

Top to bottom–3 in. (largest conduit) x 6 = 18 in. + 3 in. = 21 in. Side to side–3 in. (largest conduit) x 6 = 18 in. + 3 in. = 21 in.

Example: a pull box has 1 trade size 2-inch conduit and 1 trade size 1½-inch conduit entering the top and 2 trade size 2-inch conduits on the left side. Where conductors are larger than 4 AWG and an angle (90 deg.), pull of the conductors is to be made, determine the minimum distance required from the top wall to the bottom wall.

A. 13½ inches

B. 11 inches

C. 12 inches

D. 16 inches

Answer: (A) 13½ inches.

2 in. (largest conduit) x 6 = 12 + 1½ in. = 13½ inches.

Glossary

A

Adjustable-trip circuit breakers: circuit breakers whose trip setting can be changed by adjusting the ampere rating, trip time characteristics, or both, within a particular range.

Aluminum wire: an electrical conductor composed of aluminum metal.

Ambient temperature: the surrounding temperature present in a specific area.

American Wire Gauge (AWG): standard used to identify the size of a wire.

Ampacity: the maximum current in amperes that a conductor can carry continuously, under the conditions of use without exceeding its temperature rating.

Ampere: the unit of the current measurement. The amount of current that will flow through a one-ohm resistor when one volt is applied.

Appliance: utilization of equipment installed to perform one or more functions such as clothes washing, air conditioning, cooking, etc.

Appliance branch circuit: a branch circuit that supplies energy to one or more outlets to which appliances are to be connected.

Arc-Fault Circuit Interrupter (AFCI): a device intended to protect from the effects of arc faults by recognizing characteristics unique to arcing and functioning to de-energize the circuit when an arc fault is detected.

Automatic: performing a function without the necessity of human intervention.

B

Balanced load: the load of an electrical system in which two or more branches are balanced and symmetrical concerning voltage and intensity of the current.

Ballast: an electrical circuit component used with discharge lighting luminaires to provide the voltage necessary to strike the mercury arc within the lamp and limit the amount of current that flows through the lamp. (Examples of discharge lighting luminaires are fluorescent and HID lighting fixtures.)

Bare conductor: a conductor with no insulation or covering of any type.

Bonded (Bonding): connected to establish electrical continuity and conductivity.

Bonding conductor: the conductor connects the non-current carrying parts of electrical equipment, cable raceways, or other enclosures to the approved system ground conductor.

Bonding jumper: a conductor used to assure the required electrical connection between metal parts of an electrical system.

Bonding jumper, system: the connection between the grounded circuit conductor and the supply-side bonding jumper, the equipment grounding conductor, or both, at a separately derived system.

Box: a metallic or nonmetallic electrical enclosure used to house utilization equipment and devices, the support of luminaires, and pulling or terminating conductors.

Branch circuit: that portion of a wiring system beyond the final overcurrent protection device protecting the circuit and the outlet(s).

Branch circuit, multiwire: a branch circuit consisting of two or more ungrounded conductors with a voltage between them, and a grounded conductor with an equal voltage between it and each ungrounded conductor of the circuit and that is connected to the neutral or grounded conductor of the system.

Branch circuit rating: the ampere rating or setting of the overcurrent device protecting the conductors.

Building: a stand-alone structure or a structure that is separated from adjoining structures by firewalls.

Buried cable: a cable laid directly in the ground without being enclosed or protected in an electrical conduit.

Bus: a conductor, or group of conductors, that serves as a common connection for two or more circuits.

Busway: a sheet metal enclosure containing factory-assembled aluminum or copper busbars supported on insulators.

C

Cable: one or more insulated or non-insulated wires used to conduct electrical current.

Cable assembly: a flexible assembly containing multi conductors with a protective outer sheath.

Cablebus: an assembly of insulated conductors and terminations in an enclosed, ventilated protective metal housing.

Cable tray system: an assembly of sections and associated fittings that form a rigid structural system used to support cables and raceways.

Carrying capacity: the maximum current strength in amperes that a conductor can safely carry continuously. (See ampacity)

Celsius: a unit of measurement in degrees for the temperature at which the freezing point is 0 and the boiling point is 100. It is commonly represented by the letter "C."

Circuit: a complete path over which an electric current can flow.

Circuit breaker: a device that opens and closes circuits by nonautomatic means and opens circuits automatically when a predetermined overcurrent exists.

Continuous duty: operation at a substantially constant load for an indefinitely long time.

Continuous load: a load in which the maximum current may continue for three hours or more.

Controller: a device or group of devices that serves to govern in some predetermined manner the electric power delivered to the apparatus to which it is connected.

Control panel: a panel containing switches and other protective, controlling, and measuring devices for electrical equipment, motors, and machinery.

Copper: a brownish-red, malleable, ductile, metallic element that is an excellent conductor of electricity and heat. The most common element used for conductors in the electrical industry.

Copper wire: an electrical conductor composed of copper metal.

Cord: a small cable, very flexible, and substantially insulated to withstand wear. There is no sharp dividing line in respect to the size between a cord and a cable. Likewise, there is no sharp dividing line in respect to the insulation character between a cord and a stranded wire.

Cordand-plug connected appliance*: an appliance to be connected to the power source using a supply cord.

Cord-connected unit*: a unit intended for connection to the power source by means of a supply cord to prevent vibration or enable the unit to be moved.

Cross-section: a cutting or piece of something cut off at right angles to an axis. The cross-sectional area is 100% of the cross-section.

Current: the flow of electricity in a circuit, measured in amperes. Represented by the letter "I" or "A."

Current transformer (CT): an instrument transformer with a primary winding in series with a current-carrying conductor and a secondary winding connected to a meter or device which is actuated by conductor current and current changes.

D

Demand factor: the ratio of the maximum demand of a system or part of a system to the total connected load of a system or the part of the system under consideration. All the loads of a system are usually never used simultaneously due to the many uses of the power.

Device box*: a box that houses an electrical device(s), such as receptacles and switches.

Device: electrical components such as receptacles, switches, and dimmers that are designed to carry and control electric energy as its principal function, but do not use electricity.

Disconnecting means: a device, or group of devices, by which the circuit conductors are disconnected from their source of supply.

Double pole: switch or device connected to both lines of a circuit or controlling both lines of a circuit.

Dry location: a location not normally subject to dampness or wetness. A location classified as dry may be temporarily subject to dampness or wetness, as in a building under construction.

Duty cycle: the time interval occupied by a device on intermittent duty in starting, running, stopping, and idling.

Dwelling: a structure containing eating, living, and sleeping space and permanent provisions for cooking and sanitation.

Dwelling unit: a dwelling with one or more rooms used by one or more people for housekeeping.

E

Effectively grounded: grounded with sufficient low impedance and current-carrying capacity to prevent hazardous voltage build-ups.

Efficiency: the ratio of output power to input power, expressed as a percentage.

Electrical discharge luminaire: a luminaire (lighting fixture) that utilizes a ballast for the lamp's operation.

Electrical metallic tubing (EMT): a lightweight tubular steel raceway used for enclosed conductors.

Electric circuit: the complete path of an electric current.

Electric power production and distribution network: power production, distribution, and utilization equipment and facilities, such as electric utility systems that deliver electric power to the connected loads, are external to and not controlled by an interactive system.

Electric sign: a fixed, stationary, or portable self-contained, electrically illuminated, utilization equipment with words or symbols designed to convey information or attract attention.

Electrode: a conducting substance through which electric current enters or leaves.

Enclosed: surrounded by a case, housing, fence, or walls which will prevent persons from accidentally contacting energized parts.

Enclosure: the case or housing of equipment or other apparatus which protects live or energized parts.

Equipment: a general term including devices, luminaires, appliances, materials, machinery, apparatus, etc. used in conjunction with electrical installations.

Equipment bonding jumper: a conductor that connects two or more parts of the equipment grounding conductor.

Equipment grounding conductor: an electrical conductor provides a low-impedance path between electrical equipment and enclosures and the system grounded conductor and grounding electrode conductor.

F

Fahrenheit: a unit of measurement in degrees for the temperature at which the freezing point is 32 and the boiling point is 212. It is commonly represented by the letter "F."

Fault: an electrical defect.

Fault current: any current that travels an unwanted path, other than the normal operating path of an electrical system.

Feeder: all circuit conductors between the service equipment or the source of a separately derived system and the final branch-circuit overcurrent device.

Feeder neutral load: the maximum unbalanced load between any of the ungrounded conductors and the grounded conductor of a feeder.

Fished: a means of installing electrical wiring in existing inaccessible hollow spaces of buildings with minimum damage to the building finish.

Fixed appliance: an appliance that is fastened in place or otherwise secured at a specific location.

Fixed equipment: equipment intended to be permanently connected electrically and not easily moved.

Flexible cord: an assembly of two or more insulated conductors, with or without braids, contained within an overall outer covering and used for the connection of equipment to a power source.

Flexible metal conduit (FMC): a raceway consisting of metal strips that are formed into a circular cross-sectional raceway, which is used to enclose conductors.

Fluorescent light: a method of lighting that makes use of ultraviolet energy to activate a fluorescent material coated inside of the bulb's surface.

Full load amperes (FLA): the amount of current, in amperes, in an electrical circuit when the load is operating in a full-capacity condition.

Full load current (FLC): the motor's current required to produce the full load torque at the motor's rated speed.

Fuse: a protective device with a fusible element that opens the circuit by melting when subjected to excessive current.

G

Galvanizing: the process of coating metals with zinc to prevent corrosion.

Ganged switch box: a box containing more than one switch.

General lighting: lighting designed to provide a substantially uniform level of illumination throughout an area, exclusive of any provision for special local requirements.

General-purpose branch circuit: a branch circuit that supplies several outlets for lighting and appliances.

General-use snap switch: a form of general-use switch constructed to be installed in device and outlet boxes.

General-use switch: a switch for use in general distribution and branch circuits. The ampere rated switch is capable of interrupting its rated current at its rated voltage.

General-use receptacle: 125-volt, single-phase, 15 or-20 ampere receptacles connected to a branch circuit supplying two or more receptacles provided for the purpose of supplying cordand-plug connected loads. Not provided for specific loads such as small appliances or laundry equipment.

Generator: a device that is used to convert mechanical energy to electrical energy.

Grade: the final level or elevation of the earth at a given location.

Ground: a conducting connection between electrical circuits or equipment and the earth.

Grounded (Grounding): connected to the earth or a conducting body connected to the earth.

Grounding: the connection of all exposed non-current carrying metal parts to the earth.

Grounding conductor: a conductor used to connect equipment or the grounded circuit of a wiring system to a grounding electrode or electrodes.

Grounding electrode: a conducting object through which a direct connection to earth is established.

Grounding electrode conductor: the conductor used to connect the system grounded conductor and the equipment to a grounding electrode or a point on the grounding electrode system.

H

Handhole enclosure: an enclosure for using in underground systems provided with an open or closed bottom and sized to allow personnel to reach into, but not enter, to install, operate, or maintaining equipment or wiring or both.

Health care facility: a location, either a building or a portion of a building, containing occupancies such as hospitals, nursing homes, limited or supervisory care facilities, clinics, medical and dental offices, and either ambulatory facilities.

Hermetic refrigerant motor compressor: a combination of a compressor and motor enclosed in the same housing, having no external shaft or shaft seals, with the engine operating in the refrigerant.

Hickey (fitting): a fitting used to mount a lighting fixture in an outlet box or on a pipe or stud. It has openings through which fixture wires may be brought out of the fixture stem.

HID lamp: a high-intensity discharge lamp.

High-intensity discharge (HID) luminaire: a luminaire (lighting fixture) that generates light from an arc lamp contained within an outer tube.

Horsepower (hp): a unit of power equal to 746 watts that describes electric motors' output.

Hybrid system: a system comprised of multiple power sources. These power sources may include photovoltaic, wind, micro-hydro generators, engine-driven generators, and others, but do not have electrical production and distribution network systems. Energy storage systems, such as batteries, do not constitute a power source for this definition.

I

Identified: recognized as suitable for the use, purpose, etc.

Illumination: the supplying of light or lighting up a given area. The density of light flux projected on a surface, measured in foot-candles (FC).

Impedance: the total opposition to the flow of current in an ac circuit.

Incandescent lamp: a lamp in which the light is produced by a filament of conducting material contained in a vacuum and heated to incandescence by an electric current.

Instantaneous: a qualifying term used in giving properties and characteristics of apparatus indicating that no delay is purposely introduced in its action. Done in an instant.

Instantaneous-trip circuit breakers: circuit breakers with no delay between the fault or overload sensing element and the device's tripping action.

Insulated: separated from other conducting surfaces by a dielectric substance or air space permanently offering high resistance to the passage of current and to disruptive discharge through the meaning of space.

Insulated conductor: a conductor covered with a material identified as electrical insulation.

Intensity of current: the strength of an electric current. It is the quantity of electricity that flows past any point in a circuit in one second. It is measured by an ampere unit. Represented by the letter "I."

Interactive system: a solar photovoltaic system that operates parallel with and may deliver power to an electrical production and distribution network. For this definition, an energy storage subsystem of a solar photovoltaic system, such as a battery, is not another electrical production source.

Intermittent duty: operation for alternate intervals of (1) load and no-load; or (2) load and rest; or (3) load, no-load, and rest. A requirement of operation or service consisting of alternate periods of limitation and rest so apportioned and regulated that the temperature rise at no time exceeds that specified for the particular class of apparatus under consideration.

Intermittent load: a load in which the maximum current does not continue for three hours.

Interrupt: to stop a process in such a way that it can be resumed.

Interrupting rating: the maximum rating in amperes of an overcurrent protective device (OCPD).

Intersystem bonding termination: a device that provides a means for connecting bonding conductors for communications systems to the grounding electrode system.

Inverse-time circuit breakers: circuit breakers with an intentional delay between the time when the fault or overload is sensed and the time when the circuit breaker operates. The greater the surplus, the less time the circuit breaker takes to trip. Conversely, the smaller the overload, the more time the circuit breaker takes to trip.

J

Junction box: a box in which splices, taps, or terminations are made.

K

Kcmil: one thousand circular mils. Conductor sizes from 250 kcmil through 2,000 kcmil are expressed in this manner.

Kilo: a prefix often used with a physical unit to designate a quantity one thousand times as great. Designated by the letter "K."

Kilovolt amperes (kva): one thousand (1,000) volt-amperes.

Kilowatt (kW): one thousand (1,000) watts.

L

Lamp: a light source. Reference is to a light bulb, rather than a lamp.

Lamp holders: devices designed to accommodate a lamp for the purpose of illumination.

Lighting outlet: an outlet intended for the direct connection of a lamp holder, a lighting fixture (luminaire), or pendant cord terminating in a lamp holder.

Lighting outlets: outlets that provide power for lighting fixtures (luminaires).

Load: the amount of electric power used by any electrical unit or appliance at any given moment.

Location, damp: partially protected locations under canopies, marquees, roofed open porches, and like locations and interior locations subject to moderate degrees of moisture, such as some basements, barns, and cold storage warehouses.

Location, dry: a location not normally subject to dampness or wetness. A location classified as dry may be temporarily subject to dampness or wetness, as in the case of a building under construction.

Location, wet: installations underground or in concrete slabs or masonry, in direct contact with the earth and locations subject to saturation with water or other liquids, such as vehicle washing areas and locations exposed to weather and unprotected.

Locked rotor current: the steady-state current taken from the line with the rotor locked and with rated voltage applied to the motor.

Luminaire: a complete lighting fixture consisting of the lamp or lamps, reflector, or other parts to distribute the light, lamp guards, and lamp power supply.

M

Main bonding jumper: the connection at the service equipment that bonds together the equipment grounding conductor, the grounded conductor, and the grounding electrode conductor.

Maximum: the greatest value in any given group. A value is greater than any which precedes or follows it in a succession of values.

Metal wireway: a sheet metal raceway with a hinged or removable cover that houses and protects wires and cables laid in place after the wireway has been installed.

Mil: one-thousandths of an inch (0.001").

Mobil home: a transportable factory assembled structure or structures constructed on a permanent chassis for using as a dwelling. A mobile home is not constructed on a permanent foundation but is connected to the required utilities. The term "mobile home" does not include manufactured homes.

Module: a complete, environmentally protected unit consisting of solar cells, optics, and other components, exclusive of the tracker, designed to generate dc power when exposed to sunlight.

Motor: a device for converting electrical energy into mechanical energy.

Motor starter: an electrically operated switch (contactor) that includes overload protection.

Multiconductor cable: it consists of a number of individually insulated wires, either solid or stranded, which may or may not be grouped together within an outer covering. Sometimes an outer sheath of aluminum or steel is placed over the cable.

Multifamily dwelling: a dwelling with three or more dwelling units.

Multioutlet assembly: a metal raceway with factory-installed conductors and attachment plugs receptacles. Usually surface mounted.

Multiwire branch circuit: a branch circuit with two or more ungrounded conductors having a potential difference between them, and is connected to the neutral or grounded conductor of the system.

N

Nameplate: a plaque giving the manufacturer's name, current rating, and voltage of a transformer, generator, motor, appliance, etc.

Neutral: neither positive nor negative, having zero potential, having electrical potential intermediate between the potentials of other associated parts of the circuit, positive with reference to some parts, negative with reference to others.

Nipple: a short piece of conduit or tubing having a length not exceeding 24 inches.

Nonlinear load: a load where the wave shape of the steady-state current does not follow the wave shape of the applied voltage. Examples of nonlinear loads are electronic equipment, such as computers and HID and fluorescent lighting.

O

Ohm: the unit of measurement of electrical resistance. One ohm of resistance will allow one ampere of current to flow through pressure of one volt.

Ohm's law: a law that describes the mathematical relationship between voltage, current, and resistance.

One-family dwelling: a dwelling with one dwelling unit.

Outlet: any point in the electrical system where current supplies utilization equipment.

Overcurrent: any current in excess of that for which the conductor or equipment is rated. It may result from overload, short circuit, or ground fault.

Overload: operation of equipment in excess of normal, full-load rating, or of a conductor in excess of its rated ampacity that, when it persists for a sufficient length of time, would cause damage or dangerous overheating. A fault, such as a short circuit or ground fault, is not an overload.

Overload protection: a device that prevents overloading a circuit or motor such as a fuse or circuit breaker.

P

Panelboard: a single panel or group of assembled panels with buses and overcurrent devices, which may have switches to control light, heat, or power circuits.

Parallel conductors: two or more conductors that are electrically connected at both ends to form a single conductor.

Pendants: hanging luminaires (lighting fixtures), that use flexible cords to support the lamp holder.

Permanently-connected appliance: a hard-wired appliance that is not cordand-plug connected.

Permanently installed swimming pool: a pool constructed in-ground or partially above ground and designed to hold over 42 inches of water and all indoor pools regardless of depth.

Phase: used in ac terminology, refers basically to time. Usually, the phase position is defined by specifying the number of electrical degrees between the phase and the reference position. The number of electrical degrees that two quantities are out of phase is called the phase angle.

Phase conductor: the conductors other than the neutral conductor.

Phase converter: an electrical device that converts single-phase power to three-phase power.

Phase-to-ground voltage: the maximum voltage between any two phases of an electrical distribution system.

Portable appliance: an appliance that is actually moved or can be easily moved from one place to another in normal use.

Power (watts): a basic unit of electrical energy, measured in watts. Power is usually expressed as the letter "P" or "W."

Premises wiring: basically, all interior and exterior wiring is installed on the load side of the service point or the source of a separately derived system.

Primary: the part of a motor or transformer having windings that are connected to the power supply line.

Primary current: the current in the primary of a transformer.

Primary winding: the coil of a transformer that is energized from a source of alternating voltage and current. The input sides.

Pull box: a box used as a point to pull or feed electrical conductors in the raceway system.

R

Rated current: the load, in amperes, that a circuit breaker is intended to carry continuously without opening of the circuit.

Raceway: a metal or nonmetallic channel for enclosing and protecting conductors.

Receptacle outlets: outlets that provide power for cordand-plug connected equipment.

Rigid metal conduit (RMC): a conduit used to enclose conductors, made of metal with a galvanized protective coating.

Rigid nonmetallic conduit (RNC): a conduit made of materials other than metal, usually polyvinyl chloride (PVC).

S

Secondary current: the current induced in the secondary of a transformer or induction coil.

Separately derived system: a premises wiring system whose power is derived from a source of electric energy or equipment other than a service. Examples of separately derived systems are transformers, generators, and storage batteries. Such systems have no direct connection from circuit conductors of one system to circuit conductors of another system, other than connections through the earth, metal enclosures, metallic raceways, or equipment grounding conductors.

Series circuit: a circuit supplying energy to a number of loads connected in series. The same current passes through each load in completing its path to the source of supply.

Service: the conductors and equipment for delivering electric energy from the serving utility to the wiring system of the premises served.

Service conductors: the conductors from the service point or other source of power to the service disconnecting means.

Service drop: the overhead service conductors that extend from the last pole of the utility supply system to the service entrance conductors at the building or structure.

Service entrance cable (SE): a single or multiconductor assembly with or without an overall covering.

Service entrance conductors: conductors that connect the service equipment for the building or structure with the electrical utility supply conductors.

Service mast: an assembly consisting of a service raceway, guy wires or braces, service head, and any fittings necessary for the support of service drop conductors.

Sheath: the final outer protective coating applied to a cable.

Short circuit: the unintentional connection of two ungrounded conductors that have a potential difference between them. The condition that occurs when two ungrounded conductors (hot wires), or an ungrounded and grounded conductor of a circuit, come in contact with each other.

Short circuit protection: any automatic current-limiting system that enables a power supply to continue operating at a limited current. and without damage, into any output overload including short circuits.

Show window: any window used or designed to be used for the display of goods, products, services, or advertising material. Usually visible by the general public from street or floor level.

Single-phase: a term applied to a simple alternating current of uniform frequency as distinguished from polyphase currents.

Single-phase circuit: an ac circuit consisting of two or three intentionally interrelated conductors.

Solar cell: the basic photovoltaic device that generates electricity when exposed to light.

Special permission: the written approval of the authority having jurisdiction.

Splice: a joint used for connecting conductors together.

Stationary appliance: a cord-connected appliance that is intended to be fastened in place or located in a dedicated space.

Switch: a device, with a current and voltage rating, used to open or close an electrical circuit.

Switchboard: a single panel or group of assembled panels with buses, overcurrent devices, and instruments.

T

Thermal protection: refers to an electrical device that has inherent protection from overheating. Typically, in the form of a bimetal strip that bends when heated to a certain point.

Three-phase circuit: a combination of circuits energized by ac that differ in phase by one-third of a cycle, which is 120 degrees.

Three-phase power: a combination of three alternating currents (usually denoted as a, b and c) in a circuit with their voltages displaced 120 degrees or one-third of a cycle.

Three-phase transformer: a combination in one unit of 3 single-phase transformers with separate electric circuits, but having certain magnetic circuits in common. There are three magnetic circuits through the core and the fluxes in the various circuits are displaced in phase.

Time delay fuse: fuses designed to provide a time interval upon detection of an overload, before blowing. This type of fuse is used primarily for overcurrent protection for motors.

Transformer: an electrical device that contains no moving parts, which converts or "transforms" electrical power at one voltage or current to another voltage or current.

Transformer vault: an isolated enclosure either above or below ground, with fire-resistant walls, ceiling, and floor, for unattended transformers.

U

Unfinished basement: the portion of an area of a basement that is not intended as a habitable room, but is limited to storage areas, work areas, etc.

Ungrounded: a system, circuit, or apparatus without an intentional connection to the ground except through potential indicating or measuring devices or other very high impedance devices.

Uninterruptible power supply: a power supply used to provide alternating current power to a load for some period of time in the event of a power failure.

Utilization equipment: any electrical equipment which uses electrical energy for electronic, mechanical, heating, lighting, or similar purposes.

V

Ventilated: provided with a means to permit circulation of air sufficient to remove an excess of heat, fumes, or vapors.

Volt: the practical unit of electric pressure. The pressure will produce a current of one ampere against a resistance of one ohm.

Voltage: the greatest root-mean-square (effective) difference of potential between any two conductors or the circuit concerned.

Voltage drop: the drop of pressure in an electric circuit due to the resistance of the conductor. This loss exists in every circuit. It is directly proportional to the length of the conductor and is inversely proportional to its cross-sectional area.

Voltage, nominal: a nominal value assigned to a circuit or system for the purpose of A nominal value assigned to a circuit or system for the purpose of volts. The actual voltage at which a circuit operates can vary from the nominal within a range that permits satisfactory operation of equipment.

Voltage-to-ground: the difference of potential between a given conductor and ground.

Voltampere: the voltampere is the apparent power in an ac circuit. Represented by the letters "VA."

W

Wall-mounted oven: an oven for cooking purposes designed for mounting in or on a wall or other surface and consisting of one or more heating elements.